Ghost Hunting

A Beginner's Guide To Investigating Paranormal Activity

Basics of Paranormal Investigation, Ghost Hunting Equipment, Tips and Tricks of the Trade, Ethics of Paranormal Investigation, Ghost Hunting Techniques and More!

By Riley Star

Copyrights and Trademarks

All rights reserved. No part of this book may be reproduced or transformed in any form or by any means, graphic, electronic, or mechanical, including photocopying, recording, taping, or by any information storage retrieval system, without the written permission of the author.

This publication is Copyright ©2020. Nevada. All products, graphics, publications, software and services mentioned and recommended in this publication are protected by trademarks. In such instance, all trademarks & copyright belong to the respective owners. For information consult www.NRBpublishing.com

Disclaimer and Legal Notice

This product is not legal, medical, or accounting advice and should not be interpreted in that manner. You need to do your own due-diligence to determine if the content of this product is right for you. While every attempt has been made to verify the information shared in this publication, neither the author, neither publisher, nor the affiliates assume any responsibility for errors, omissions or contrary interpretation of the subject matter herein. Any perceived slights to any specific person(s) or organization(s) are purely unintentional.

We have no control over the nature, content and availability of the web sites listed in this book. The inclusion of any web site links does not necessarily imply a recommendation or endorse the views expressed within them. We take no responsibility for, and will not be liable for, the websites being temporarily unavailable or being removed from the internet.

The accuracy and completeness of information provided herein and opinions stated herein are not guaranteed or warranted to produce any particular results, and the advice and strategies, contained herein may not be suitable for every individual. Neither the author nor the publisher shall be liable for any loss incurred as a consequence of the use and application, directly or indirectly, of any information presented in this work. This publication is designed to provide information in regard to the subject matter covered. Neither the author nor the publisher assume any responsibility for any errors or omissions, nor do they represent or warrant that the ideas, information, actions, plans, suggestions contained in this book is in all cases accurate. It is the reader's responsibility to find advice before putting anything written in this book into practice. The information in this book is not intended to serve as legal, medical, or accounting advice.

Foreword

A "Ghost" is usually defined as nothing more than a solar spirit that has left the human body and it's still here. Different religions or spiritual beliefs will put us in different directions to what happens to that ghost but the general generic term if you're watching a movie or reading a book, you would understand what a ghost is, and it's often associated with eeriness. However, it doesn't satisfies everyone's palette because what if the "ghost" is not a person or even an animal since an animal has a solar spirit that also leaves the body, what if it's a large ship that appears and disappears? What if it's a phantom car? Wherein there's no soul or spirit there, which is why the generic term, definition or description of a ghost just doesn't work; we have to come up with better ideas and perhaps broaden our perspectives.

Needless to say, the spectrum of what a ghost is has to expand just like how it is any philosophical or scientific pursuit. There's no such thing as absolute. Are you ready to hunt some ghosts?

Table of Contents

Introduction: Paranormal Philosophy 1

Chapter One: What is a Ghost? 2

    The Conscious Energy Theory 3

    The Multiple Personality Disorder Theory 7

    Residual Energy 10

    The Holographic Principle Theory 14

Chapter Two: Ghost Hunting Equipment 16

    Basic Equipments 17

Chapter Three: Paranormal Investigations and Research 24

    Paranormal Investigations 25

        Dealing with Children as an Eye Witness 28

    Paranormal Research 33

Chapter Four: How to Use the Scientific Method in Ghost Hunting 42

    What is a Scientific Method? 43

Chapter Five: Ethics of Paranormal Investigation 48

    Deception 50

Chapter Six: Paranormal Investigation Proper 52

    Classification of Ghosts 54

    Tips Before Leaving the House 56

    Ghost Haunting Basics 61

    Arrival on Location 66

Chapter Seven: Paranormal Investigation Techniques 68

    Be a Skeptic and Do Some Debunking First 69

Chapter Eight: EVP Sessions 74

    Capturing EVPs 75

    Sample Questions to Ask 78

    Classification of EVPs 80

Chapter Nine: Additional Ghost Hunting Tips 84

    Photo and Video Tips 86

    Tricks of the Trade 88

Chapter Ten: Prayers of Protection 92

    Prayers Before the Investigation 93

    Prayers After the Investigation 95

    Protection Prayers 98

Glossary of Paranormal Terms 104

Index 110

PHOTO REFERENCES 112

REFERENCES 114

Introduction: Paranormal Philosophy

In this book, we will discuss a more in depth look of the subjects related to the paranormal field whether we're talking about ghosts, haunted houses and why they're haunted, the equipment that paranormal investigators use, and paranormal activities in general. We will also look at the theories that are out there and the other ideas that people have about a certain paranormal phenomenon.

Introduction: Paranormal Philosophy

Paranormal is for me a form of philosophy. We will delve deeper in different subjects that have to do with the reality, existence and knowledge in the paranormal field. It's very important to understand that when it comes to philosophy, we agree to disagree. After all, philosophy is all about bringing all ideas regardless if you agree with them or not. However, as you know these ideas whether they are good or not contributes to creating theories that can be proven or become a reality. This is the reason why it's important to lay out the foundation.

The paranormal field is labeled as pseudoscience, it's usually not taken seriously and that's probably because it never had a philosophy which means there's no foundation and it attributes its basis off of mystic beliefs, ancient religions and word – of – mouth but no one actually took an in – depth look at it because there's a lot of factors involved like scam artists and whatnot that eventually destroyed the field.

In the next few chapters we're going to talk about the most familiar subject in the world of the paranormal –

Introduction: Paranormal Philosophy

ghosts. You're going to learn what a ghost is and also the different subject matters in line with it.

Introduction: Paranormal Philosophy

Chapter One: What is a Ghost?

This is something that Jason Sullivan, a paranormal expert, talked about. He came up with this idea after reading Dr. Robert Becker and Gary Sheldon's book called *The Body Electric*. The book discusses about the human consciousness, our body's frequency, and man's existence.

Chapter One: What is a Ghost?

The Conscious Energy Theory

Jason Sullivan's Conscious Energy Theory is that when a person dies, the consciousness struggles to survive. After the body has died, the consciousness extends itself out and latches on to any available energy in its environment to pull itself together and keep itself "alive" and that creates a conscious energy, or what we refer to as a ghost. So the more energy is available, the longer it can spend and draw in more having left it with more memory. The stronger the energy, the stronger the conscious energy. The energy that's available in the environment could be electric, electromagnetic, electrostatic, electrochemical or even nuclear.

This idea that Jason Sullivan came up with can be applied to people, animals and other sources of energy. Based on Sullivan's experience with people especially those who have had an "Out – of – Body Experience" (OBE), and what happens to these patients during the time they were unconscious or chemically induced for a major operation is very interesting because they tell the same experience. I'm sure you've heard from other people, or seen it from movies.

Chapter One: What is a Ghost?

So, what Sullivan learned from these patients during the time that they were unconscious is that, they were floating out of their bodies (during a surgery or while their body is shut - down) and they were leaving the room and some people even described that they were in the roof or sort of overlooking the whole room and have a bird's eye view of everything to which they can see it all happening at the same time. The amazing thing that Sullivan discovered is that these patients while having these paranormal experiences is that they still felt tethered to the body or attached to it like a balloon. They float, they can see everything but they were immediately drawn back in to their bodies. So from there, according to Sullivan, there's no difference when it comes to an unconscious person having an out – of – body experience to a ghost because the energy signatures are the exact same thing. It's both consciousness floating around but the only difference is that the conscious energy of a ghost is not attached anymore to a living body.

You see, we are bio – chemical electrical machines. Your consciousness develops from the moment you were born, it has self – awareness and it will strive to survive. The real question is when a conscious energy is created, how

Chapter One: What is a Ghost?

strong can it be? And how much consciousness or memory can it retain?

In a conscious energy situation where you are performing an electronic voice phenomenon sessions trying to communicate with a ghost; in theory, electronic voice phenomenon is when the ghost tries to communicate with us using the electromagnetic spectrum because that's where all the energy frequencies generate. However, it's often limited to its responses and that's probably because the investigator is not asking the right questions, or perhaps when that consciousness is created, it only takes in all that it can but it might not take in the answers to the questions we ask.

This is why I highly encourage you to be broad and not have to ask only a set of questions, sometimes you have to talk and see where that will lead you. So basically what the conscious energy theory explains that the more energy available, the more the consciousness has the power to reply. Sometimes it's very little and sometimes it's very powerful. It will also depend on how much energy it gathered for the first time it was created or as it was being created, the more

Chapter One: What is a Ghost?

energy it already pulled in, it may be able to interact with its environment.

Black Shadows

People who have had paranormal experiences sometimes describe seeing a "black shadows." This black shadows moves across the walls in a smooth and sleek way, and it is visible to the eye. Sometimes it is compose of dust or particles from a debris. So for instance, we have a conscious energy that's electromagnetic, then it would appear like a dust – cloud as it will pick up fine particles of dirt and debris and as it would move along you will see a black shadows.

This is why paranormal investigators use night vision cameras during a ghost hunt because of the electromagnetism that you may have static discharges as a conscious energy tries to move in its environment. With those black shadows moving around, it's very possible that this conscious energy of ours is a electrostatic but it's no different than any other ghost, it just has a little bit more power and perhaps quite stronger, and because of that its electromagnetic field is strong enough that it's collecting dust, dirt or debris. Again, this is all part of paranormal philosophy. As Jason Sullivan stated, it's all part of a theory as it lays the foundation for a much deeper understanding of the paranormal world.

The Multiple Personality Disorder Theory

There's another theory that Jason Sullivan came up with which is truly fascinating. It came from the concept laid out by an anesthesiologist named Dr. Stewart Hammeroff. Hammeroff had a scientific theory called the Quantum Consciousness. He referred to the brain as a quantum computer but more importantly, he talks about the knowledge and consciousness that always exists in one's reality – mapped environment. It's a three – dimensional image that surrounds us all the time and due to entanglement, it's always available to be grasps and pulled back in just like what we've talked about in the OBE earlier.

So when it comes to a conscious energy or a ghost, and you take the theory of Dr. Hammeroff's Quantum Consciousness, you will find that they are align with one another. According to Sullivan, the fact that a consciousness can exist outside the body and can gather or pull in information, keep it and be able to interact with its environment and how paranormal investigators can review that information from the conscious energy once it's captured during their interactions with the paranormal provides a valuable concept in the way we understand the nature of ghosts.

The Quantum Consciousness theory will take us into a completely different realm because we're talking about using real science to explain paranormal theories but as Sullivan points out, we have to create the theories first, expand our horizon and lay the foundation of paranormal philosophy.

From the concepts of Quantum Consciousness comes Sullivan's Multiple Personality Disorder Theory. It's derived from Dr. Hammeroff when he talked about the possibility of a consciousness finding itself another host. According to Hammeroff, this can help explain the concept of reincarnation and the likes. Jason Sullivan extracted that idea and come up with Multiple Personality Disorder

Chapter One: What is a Ghost?

Theory. He wondered what if the consciousness will find an attraction to a similar frequency? Also taking in from the concepts he learned from The Body Electric where humans have its own magnetic field and frequency then it's quite possible that a conscious energy can be attracted to a similar frequency and let it be absorb into the new host whether it is a human, an animal or a certain object.

The multiple personality disorder is a real thing and science has proven it through examining the neuro – pathways or the brain wave scan of patients with multiple personality disorder, scientists found out that each personality is completely different or the brain waves being emitted is different from one another. So for instance, there's a person named Mark with a certain set of personality, say he's someone that doesn't smoke, then suddenly changes a personality to someone who loves to smoke, if you scan the brain waves for each of the personality type it actually changes. Needless to say, it's the same body but operating a different consciousness – the Mark who loves to smoke, and the Mark who doesn't.

Chapter One: What is a Ghost?

This can also be applied to people who believed that they have a past life, and those who suddenly have knowledge that they've never had. Jason Sullivan's theory is about a conscious energy that was absorbed into another host because it has the same level of frequency or vibration. According to him, it's also possible that the conscious energy that found another host doesn't want to be dominant but it stays there, and gives the host dreams or knowledge that didn't belong to him/ her. It can create a series of dejavu as one go to places they haven't been before but the other consciousness already has.

Residual Energy

Residual Energy is something that can also be referred to as spiritual imprinting. So for instance, let's say you have a computer monitor and you left it there for a long time then change it, you can notice that it left behind an imprint or a silhouette that is still visible; this is the same with spiritual imprinting.

As mentioned earlier, objects like ships, cars, dolls etc. can sometimes show up as ghost as how it is portrayed in

Chapter One: What is a Ghost?

most TV shows, or even taken from those who have had a paranormal experience but really it's just residual energy or spiritual imprinting that left its mark in the paranormal field. If something exists long enough, it's very possible that it leaves an energy signature in the ether.

For example, there are paranormal investigators who have done investigations in subdivisions where people claim that they've heard a train. According to the residents, some of them actually saw it, and even hear or felt it because it literally shook their walls whenever it passes by as if it actually exists. The thing though is that there are no train tracks; in fact there haven't been in 20 years.

However, through further research, paranormal investigators found out that there was train tracks at one time in that area and the train ran on a consistent schedule for many decades before the area became part of the subdivision. That is an example of residual energy because the train literally left a strong residual imprint in its environment even though it already stopped running for 20 years or so. Somehow the residual energy of the train is

Chapter One: What is a Ghost?

triggered by the environment which is why residents there can hear it, feel it and even see it.

This is the same with so – called ghost ships or phantom cars, these are things that left energy signatures in their environment strong enough that it can literally affect their environment or can be triggered by it. Certain events can be triggered and parts of history may actually repeat but how the residual energy is being triggered is still up for further debate and a whole new topic concerning paranormal philosophy.

Another example of ghostly encounters that paranormal expert, Jason Sullivan shared is about a woman who has been married for 40 years, and her husband who works as a machinist everyday for 35 years. Her husband goes to work and came home from work every day at the same time for the last 35 years. The husband comes home through the side door of the house straight to their basement, takes a shower, come upstairs, greets his wife and asks her what's for dinner, goes to the living room, watch TV until his wife tells her that dinner is ready.

Chapter One: What is a Ghost?

Needless to say, the woman's husband followed a strict routine for many years then he passes away. Suddenly there's some paranormal activity happening in the house. The wife reports that the side door pops open, occasionally the shower downstairs opens, she sees the TV turning on by itself, and one time when she was sitting with her daughter – in – law and grandson, she actually heard someone yells "what's for dinner?." What's funny is that her daughter – in – law heard it too and it actually put her at ease because for the first time somebody heard it too.

After Sullivan's team is doing an investigation, it turned out that the side door always open around three o'clock which is the same time when the husband came home from work, and it's also around the time when the sun peak over the side of the house and hit the door; so putting in the environmental factor into it but also the fact that the residual energy could be triggered by the thermo energy coming from the son which pops the door open around that time. Sullivan and his team don't even to use their audio equipment because they themselves have heard "what's for dinner?" using their own ears.

Chapter One: What is a Ghost?

This is like the aforementioned example with the train; the husband lived a regiment life and left an imprint of residual energy in its environment. What Sullivan suggested to the wife if she wants it to stop is to simply break the pattern like move the furniture, put a lock on the side door, turn the water off in the shower etc. anything that will disturb the pattern and eventually the residual energy.

The Holographic Principle Theory

This is a theory created by a scientist named Leonard Sasken and it something related to the concept of residual energy, and the idea is that the events, information or knowledge is never lost and we can tap into it anytime. It shares the same theory of Dr. Hammeroff that we've talked about earlier where consciousness is always there.

The Holographic Principle Theory is a part of paranormal philosophy and a foundation of the paranormal field. The theory basically talks about how us humans can imprint ourselves in our environment including our knowledge and even our existence like the examples given earlier. The cool thing is that we can extract or tap into that certain knowledge or existence by triggering the event.

One way of triggering the event that is often used in the paranormal field is reenactments. Paranormal investigators are reenacting the environment to be exactly like it was at the time that these people/ ghosts might have existed. The interesting thing is that when reenactment happens, it triggers the event and the residual energy appears for a moment or two where people can actually see, hear or feel it with their own physical senses.

The ideas and theories you've just read are very important even if you agree to disagree with it as it provides a foundation for the paranormal science and enables paranormal investigators and experts to come up with better and stronger theories when it comes to explaining the paranormal activities that people usually experience.

Chapter Two: Ghost Hunting Equipment

In this chapter we will talk about what paranormal experts and investigators use in the field to help them along in doing their research and investigations to hunt down ghosts. We will start with the easiest equipment that you can easily acquire. Believe it or not, things like thermo – imaging cameras and other hi – tech stuff you see on TV to hunt the paranormal are not really necessary because the basic stuff can get the job done. However, if it's okay with you to spend quite a fortune for these hi – tech equipment, then by all means do it especially if you think that it can further your paranormal pursuits.

Chapter Two: Ghost Hunting Equipment

Basic Equipments

The equipments below are perfect for beginners. It won't cost you a lot and sometimes you can even get it for free if you know where to look.

Digital Camera

A digital camera is a must – have for any ghost hunter. It's a simple camera wherein you can use a 2 gigabyte memory that can store up to 1500 photos. Obviously, if you buy a much larger memory card, you can take lots of photos and evidences. If you're not the old – school type, the camera on your phone will also do.

In any paranormal investigation, one of the most essential things is to never stop taking photos. You need to take as many shots as possible. I highly suggest that you get somebody whose job is solely to take photos of you or your group whenever you are conducting a paranormal investigation.

Chapter Two: Ghost Hunting Equipment

Video Camera

Another must – have during ghost hunting investigations is a video camera. This piece of equipment is one of the most important things to use during the paranormal investigation because it is how you can actually tell your story to other people. It serves as a strong proof of what you have found and it also provide you evidence that you can review over and over again.

You can do an investigation without a digital cam but without a video camera it's much harder for you to do your job especially after the investigation. The video camera is what you will use to also relive your experience and let other people actually experienced what you've gone through in a particular ghost hunting session which is why capturing it all on video is very important.

Make sure to have it fully charged or bring an extra battery. I highly suggest that you buy long – lasting batteries that can run for around eight hours or more. The more storage space the better. You might want to also buy extra memory storage to ensure that you never miss any important footage from the actual "ghost scene."

Chapter Two: Ghost Hunting Equipment

Although the type of video cam is not that important because what's important is to just keep rolling, I still highly recommend that you use a High Definition video camera to perfectly capture whatever element is present, and also make sure to have a backup just in case technical glitches occur. Once again, it's a good idea to have members of your crew dedicated to just recording the whole thing (ideally two people or more).

You also need to remember that even when you/ your crew is on a break, you want to make sure that the camera is rolling because you never know when something is going to occur. You can also use your Smartphone to film it if you don't want the hassle of bringing video cams since most mobile gadgets now have a high video quality recording.

EMF (Electro Magnetic Field) Readers

Ideally, you want to have two pieces of EMF readers just so you can have a backup and because you want to sort of have an accurate reading. In ghost hunting or paranormal investigations, one of the main theories is that supernatural activity or paranormal presence usually conjures up

Chapter Two: Ghost Hunting Equipment

electromagnetic fields. For instance, you can be in a house, field, cemetery, or any deserted place that has absolutely no power or something that is completely away from power lines or power structures, anything that gives off power like a cell tower and the likes; what you may encounter is that your batteries and gadgets may drain, and you yourself might feel tired or nauseated – that's where the EMF reader comes in.

You see, there are no magnetic fields that are just floating around randomly; usually what happens is that a "ghost" or any form of paranormal presence concentrates its energy to become active creating a small but registered electromagnetic field which is why it's an essential tool to have during your ghost hunting sessions as it can really help you identify if a certain element or presence is there. Don't worry though, EMF readers are very easy to use, it's also cheap but very handy.

Flashlight/s

Flashlights are very important for any serious ghost hunter. You and your team should carry several flashlights

Chapter Two: Ghost Hunting Equipment

as part of your ghost hunting arsenal. The best type of flashlight to use is LED flashlight because this is a high intensity discharge lamps. LED flashlights give off the best light possible whenever you are hunting ghosts because it gives off an even flow of light (the same amount of light that a mag light gives off), and most importantly it doesn't don't leave a white dot unlike other flashlights. Whenever you use it to light the distance, it creates an illuminated field. It's also smaller, more compact and best of all you can get it for just ten bucks or so.

Thermo Reader

Another important equipment that professional paranormal investigators use is something that can measure the temperature inside a room or a home. You can use a standalone digital thermometer or better yet a thermo reader. What a thermo reader does is it easily tells you the surface temperature of anything that you point it at. It usually comes with a laser pointer so that you can exactly know what you're pointing at and also a light – up LED screen so you can see at night. What it will do for you is that

Chapter Two: Ghost Hunting Equipment

it will allow you to scan the area and give you the temperature of anything that can be coming across.

The scanning of temperature is important along with your EMF reader because it gives you an idea of pinpointing where an anomaly is, which can then help you get started.

The constant measurement of a temperature fluctuation is usually an indicator that there's a "ghostly" presence because temperature fluctuations range from 10 to 20 degrees or greater, so what you're looking for is where exactly it is constant because that means there is a concentrated energy which can also be confirmed with your EMF reader as a certain area can be completely off than other areas in the room. This works especially if you're working in a place where temperature is constant, where there is no wind or outside natural interference. You can get a thermo reader for around $40 dollars or more.

Thermo - Imaging Equipment

Again, this is not necessary especially if you are just a beginner because it is very expensive to buy but for educational purposes (and if one day you decided to

Chapter Two: Ghost Hunting Equipment

purchase one), a thermo – imaging equipment can capture the actual image of a concentrated energy which can help you and your team to easily identify where or what kind of ghost/ paranormal you are dealing with at the moment as it usually gives off a figure of that concentrated energy.

Chapter Three: Paranormal Investigations and Research

Paranormal investigations and paranormal research are two different things. In this chapter we will discuss both and see which one you might prefer implementing once you get out there on the field. You can also do both if you want to have a stronger conviction whenever you're studying or understanding a certain paranormal phenomenon.

Chapter Three: Paranormal Investigations and Research

Paranormal Investigations

This is the method where a paranormal investigator goes in the field and witness the hunt for themselves. It's very simple, somebody told you a ghost story, you go there and saw it for yourself. It's like you're a police detective on surveillance of any criminal activities.

It's very important for paranormal investigators to prepare before they do the actual investigation. There's a lot of part in the investigation that you need to do before you get to that eye witness account.

Get the general information

One of which is doing background checks on the property or location and even the people where you got a report about a paranormal activity. You may need to go through county records, get permits if you need to go inside a building (otherwise you can be sued for trespassing), find out who are the previous or current owner/s of the property, maybe you need to also learn if the land itself where it's located is a previous cemetery or built out of previous

Chapter Three: Paranormal Investigations and Research

infrastructures that can give you more information on what you will be dealing with. The most essential thing is to find out exactly who lived there, when it was built, and general information about a particular location.

Do background checks

The importance of doing background checks especially on the previous/ current owners or residents before going in is to simply keep you and your team safe. Some people say it is an invasion of privacy but if you're asked to do a paranormal investigation on a location, it's very important for you to protect yourself and your paranormal investigation team because you don't know if the location is safe and you don't know if people living there are safe.

The way that you should look at everything is you approached it fresh and whatever you are going to get yourself into should be safe for you/ your team first. You can even let the people know that you're doing background checks on them and their property.

Chapter Three: Paranormal Investigations and Research

Talk to eye witnesses

Once you have done the first two and have validated that the location is safe as well as the eye witnesses you're going to interview or interact with are safe, you can now sit down with them and get every single ghost story or paranormal activity they've experienced in a particular location. You should have eye witness accounts from everybody; if it's a family, you need to talk to all the members including the children.

Another most important thing that not a lot of investigators think about is that you have to interview each of the people involved one – on – one. If you're going to interview children, it's okay to have their parents present depending on the age of the child. You may want to get the parent/s sitting behind a child and instruct them to not say a word during the interrogation, and have the child focus on you as if their parents are not in a room.

The most important thing is that you don't want any of your ghost stories or eye witness accounts to be enhanced

Chapter Three: Paranormal Investigations and Research

or hyped which could happen when you do a group interview because they've heard of somebody else's account.

Dealing with Children as an Eye Witness

The children should be the last people you need to interview because you can get one – on – one interviews on the adults but kids shouldn't hear the stories so that once you ask the kids their stories will not be tainted from the stories of the adult. Children are usually honest when telling a story or whatever it is they've experience because they don't have a clue to make up something. When it comes to ghost accounts, children can give you the best information possible and sometimes you can even dig deeper in the child and they have an imaginary friend, and that this imaginary friend has a name, a job and there are more details to which there can already be an anomaly because that may most likely be a conscious energy or a ghost that's been interacting with that child which is why it's important to do your interview processes, be thorough, be polite and learn how you can get the child to trust you.

Chapter Three: Paranormal Investigations and Research

When you're talking to a child during the interview process, you might want to start off with questions like what their favorite video game is or they're favorite flavor before you go to harder questions. You might also do the hard questions in between the easy ones. You need to make them feel comfortable and present yourself as a friend whom they can trust if you want to successfully get information out of them.

Cross – Reference Your Eye Witness Accounts

After gathering all your stories, the next step is to cross – reference your eye witness accounts, and find out what kind of matches you have. For instance, who have been saying the exact same thing, how many accounts come up with the exact same story. Obviously, they will all tell it in different ways depending on how they've experienced it but you can pretty much get the common denominator in each of them. That's the best way to match up with the truest version of the story, and it will help you and your team on what to focus on the investigation. Take note, your

Chapter Three: Paranormal Investigations and Research

investigation and not your research because it's now your turn as an investigator to seat at the location and get an eye witness account for yourself of what the ghost hunt is; see what paranormal activity is happening there for yourself. You already have an idea based on the eye witness accounts, you know what everyone have seen, felt or heard so you know exactly what you should be seeing for yourself or what you need to find.

Now some people might argue that interviewing eye witnesses first is a bad idea because you already have a tiny bit of information, and you will automatically assume that what you will see or hear is the story that you've heard. While this is true, it's also important for you to know that that's where being a true skeptic comes in. You have to have the skill of a true skeptic. Skeptics demand proof and that's why it's a skill you can acquire while you're on the field investigating so that the information you've learned beforehand won't mislead you. That's what a true paranormal investigator is; you're not here to believe everything that other people say, and you should also be skeptic when it comes to your own thoughts because your

Chapter Three: Paranormal Investigations and Research

own brain could assume that what you've experienced is related to the ghost story you just learned even when it's not. The first part of the investigation is for you to be an eye witness yourself.

Bring minimal amount of equipment

This is another important thing to remember when you observe a paranormal activity for the first time. You don't want to disrupt the environment. This is like similar to a crime scene; you don't want to move the body or the object for awhile so you can see exactly where it fell down or the other factors involved. This is the same with paranormal investigation, except it's not after – the – fact but during.

Needless to say, you want to go in the location and try not to change anything. However, you still need to collect data because you want to have a backup of what you're about to see or hear, plus you don't want to have the ghost walk out on you without any sort of proof but you don't want to have lots of cameras. This is because whenever you're doing a paranormal investigation, the eye witnesses

Chapter Three: Paranormal Investigations and Research

that you talk to particularly when you're dealing with a residential location or business establishment, they're usually not talking about 20 rooms in the house or building being haunted, it's usually just one or two areas that a conscious energy is located in. So then you and your team are allowed to concentrate to a specific area since it's usually not the whole place.

There are a couple of things that are important when you're doing a preliminary investigation:

Remember what the witness told you

Make sure to listen to what they say and focus on it so that you won't miss out on anything. If an eye witness tells you that a particular door is slamming on its own, you need to put video cameras in there so you can have video evidence and also examine the door first. The key thing is you stay and focus on the areas that the eye witnesses talk about and be particular in details. Don't wander off somewhere else where the eye witnesses haven't talked about it being haunted.

Chapter Three: Paranormal Investigations and Research

Paranormal Research

After doing a preliminary investigation, having experienced the paranormal activity yourself, and you have evidences using your video camera or audio equipment to back it all up the next thing you need to do is to document everything and have proof as well as multiple resources to back it up before you declare that a certain location is haunted. This is where paranormal research begins. There are some people who don't do research, they just investigate and go to the next thing after they've gathered information and witness it for themselves. Needless to say, they're only there for the exciting part and can't wait to go the next place.

I highly suggest you don't do commercial haunting because if you have witness yourself a paranormal activity where an actual ghost interacts with its environment, I don't think you need to go anywhere else because that's exactly where you need to be. Unlike how it is portrayed on TV and movies, it's very hard and extremely rare to find paranormal activity where you can witness it yourself. So try not to go commercially "haunted" places if you want to find a ghost

Chapter Three: Paranormal Investigations and Research

because it's a set – up, it's all just hype. When you become a paranormal investigator and you've seen it yourself and you have data to back it up, there's where you need to be.

Data Collecting

You need to do data collecting because this is where your research starts to take place. Every single theory that you will ever come up with can be tested. If you will use an electromagnetic field whenever you're doing a paranormal investigation, you have to ask yourself first what's the purpose? Why? What's your theory? What's your team's take on using an EMF reader, a thermo reader/ thermo – imaging? Why are you going to use this kind of camera, why would you put it in a particular place?

So it's like this, the reason why you will use an EMF reader is because in theory, ghosts give off an electromagnetic field which can register in an EMF reader especially after you've done a scan of the perimeter where it is said to be haunted, and you found that there's no

Chapter Three: Paranormal Investigations and Research

grounded outlets and perhaps there's no free floating electromagnetic fields.

Once you're doing the paranormal research, all of a sudden you get these anomalies, these electromagnetic field frequencies from other parts of the room/ places that registered nothing when you did the preliminary investigation. This is the kind of paranormal activities that you need data collecting to help backup your theory.

Data collecting is also about documenting the measurement or the reading you're getting in a particular area or particular time. You may get temperature fluctuations or EMF reading fluctuations, this is why you need to mark your locations and map out everything.

Research is the part of the paranormal investigation that's hard because you have to commit and gather data and do the work to find out what the real anomaly is. Here's what it means, is what you find a conscious energy or a ghost, an actual spiritual energy, that's hanging around in that location and is it trying to communicate with you? Or does it only exist in that area and you're interaction in that

Chapter Three: Paranormal Investigations and Research

area causes something to trigger the event and communicate? You have to find out what is it, who is it (a man, woman, child?), can it give you simple information (name, what state they're from, what they do, etc.)? These questions are important as part of your research that you can ask a conscious energy so that you'll get to understand it more.

One of the stupidest questions that you often see on TV/ movies is that "can you give us a sign of your presence?" It's because if you as a living person can't even tell then how do you think a ghost is going to? Keep in mind, a ghost/ conscious energy doesn't have a brain anymore, it can't think. It only acquired the amount of information that was transferred with that new form of energy. You have better luck of asking random questions from it than to ask if it exists.

A conscious energy only has a limited amount of information that it had kept which is why you have to ask the right questions, and you're only going to find out if you ask a lot of it. It's basically hits and misses. That's the key if

Chapter Three: Paranormal Investigations and Research

you want to get a response or an interaction since you're trying to trigger the event.

So if you saw a ghost in an area, you have to record the time, what is everybody doing at that time you saw it (does your team have a cell phone on etc.), what's the temperature, if you're outside what's the moon phase, what's the weather like, what are the equipment being used and what was turned on or off etc. You want to know everything because you want to try recreating or reenacting it so that it would trigger the event and hopefully the ghost will appear again. This process is where you can apply the scientific method wherein you will have to start off with a hypothesis, keep testing it and recreate it. This is what you want do to prove your hypothesis and for paranormal research. You will always be asking the question 'why' on every single thing you do.

For instance, when you're performing an EVP (Electronic Voice Phenomena) session and you get the anomaly because let's say you ask the right question, then all of a sudden you have a response. How did that conscious

Chapter Three: Paranormal Investigations and Research

energy broadcast it to your recorder? If you're videotaping your sessions (which you should be), there are some things that can happen. For example, the microphone in your cameras and your main recorder can have a record of that, and some of the microphone/ cameras set – up might have a clearer version of that EVP which will allow you to identify where exactly the conscious energy is stronger in that area; you can easily detect it if you have the room mapped out and you know where your cameras are located by triangulating its location and you can take note of that.

Another possibility is that only a particular recorder has the EVP and none of the other equipment does. Is it possible that the ghost or the conscious energy is absorbing the piece of your equipment and draining the battery to have the power to answer your questions but it might be like it plugged itself into the recorder to give you a response which is why it wasn't picked up by your other equipment. So that's where all your wild theories can start, and there's nothing wrong with that. It's important for you to come up with your observation and your own theories.

Chapter Three: Paranormal Investigations and Research

You want to be able to tell people that when there's a ghost present, it's very possible that when they are moving in a room or if there's a very strong paranormal activity, the temperature will be hot. It will be extremely warm. You will be determined of your theory because you know that conscious energy when it's moving, it's aligned with Maxwell's theory when you have electricity, you have magnetism and all of that is creating electro – magnetic field readings and that electricity is creating heat. It's not supposed to be getting cold, it should be getting warm. This is all part of theory.

Your paranormal research is going to be a series of data collecting on anything you can ever imagine because you need to treat everything like a crime scene. You need to collect ounces of data, and things you haven't even thought of. Just like I mentioned earlier, whenever a paranormal activity happens and you go back to do your research, and let's say the event happens again, you want to note everything that just took place: what is everybody doing, the equipment you're using, what time it is, temperature, weather and other environmental factors etc.

Chapter Three: Paranormal Investigations and Research

The goal is to trigger the event again and make sure that everything is the exact same thing because if you change one thing, you may not be able to trigger it again. You want to have it all lined up the same way it was the first time. This is the difference between paranormal investigating and paranormal research.

Take your time with both and be thorough but try not to rush for one and skip the other. Don't do an investigation and go to the next place. If you want to be a true paranormal investigator, like anything else in life, you want to put in the work and do the research. If you think the research side is too much for you, then you have to make sure that there will be members of your team who are willing to do it.

Chapter Three: Paranormal Investigations and Research

Chapter Four: How to Use the Scientific Method in Ghost Hunting

In this chapter you'll learn how to apply the scientific method as it pertains to paranormal investigation. If you don't know what a scientific method is, don't worry because in the next few pages you're going to learn the processes involved and how it applies in the paranormal field and how ghost hunters are trying to step away in the field of pseudoscience.

Chapter Four: How to Use the Scientific Method in Ghost Hunting

What is a Scientific Method?

The scientific method is an account that scientists use to reliably and accurately get a constant function of the world. So for instance, if a scientist tells you how an earth rotates on its axis, he/she would be able to give you a concrete definition of hypothesis that leads to a theory which becomes the law and nature of how the earth spins.

You will use this exact same method and apply it to the paranormal field. There are four steps to the scientific method. Each of these four steps will help you become a better paranormal investigator than you are right now. This scientific process will help you in your notes, your field studies and when it comes to analyzing your findings. It will also help you get more concrete evidence instead of guesses.

Scientific Method #1: Observation

The first step is observation of the anomaly. You need to write down your evidence based on your five senses and just document it as ease. You want to also do these multiple

Chapter Four: How to Use the Scientific Method in Ghost Hunting

times and preferably with your team. An investigation that is done on the scene should be done more than five times. So wherever the location of the haunt or the paranormal activity is; you should visit it for around six times or so. In that way, each time you have a different observation and perhaps activity which can lead to a better conclusion. And then you can cross – reference your notes after the investigation and see if there's anything consistent.

Scientific Method #2: Formulate a Hypothesis

A hypothesis is an educated guess. After observing the area, the next step is to formulate an idea or a reason that you think how the occurrence is happening. For instance, if you are investigating in an old abandoned house, and you see the door slamming with nobody there, you might want to check first if the screws or the knob is loose, you might want to see if there's a wind that's coming from the window causing the door to move etc. Beyond that you can create a hypothesis (which can be in the form of maps, drawings, ideas etc.) to make a conclusion. You need to come up with

Chapter Four: How to Use the Scientific Method in Ghost Hunting

some type of theory at that moment after you've concluded all your notes through your observation. So this method is all about creating a hypothesis or coming up with a reason why the anomaly or the paranormal activity has happened.

Scientific Method #3: Test Your Hypothesis

You will have to use the hypothesis you got from watching the environment you are investigating and test it. You can test it out by recreating the event and see if it happens again. You want to see if you can predict how it will happen. So for example, you have a client and he/she tells you that the chair is moving in a particular area, and what you do is place a tape under each chair so you can mark all four corners of it, and then you come back in and you notice that the chairs have been moved; you do this over and over, and you can predict it that means that your hypothesis is sound. You also want to record all of it.

One standard rule when it comes to ghost haunting is to never stop taking notes. Make sure to have your recording devices with you either an audio or video equipment, or

Chapter Four: How to Use the Scientific Method in Ghost Hunting

your little notebook. So that's what it means to test your hypothesis. You test your idea, you do it again, keep documenting and see if you can predict it or replicate the event or the anomaly.

Scientific Method #4: Prove Your Hypothesis

This method is quite similar to method #3 but this time, you need to get more people involved not just your crew but also some experts like a mathematician, scientists, media, other folks etc. You want to show people that you have predicted this paranormal activity and that you can make it happen and show them that it is actually happening once you trigger the event. This is the final step.

You want to do this multiple times to predict it more accurately, you also need to do this for multiple sets of people, and you want to have a strong documentation of each moment. If you tell somebody that at exactly this time, the curtain will move from side to side, everyone should see it because that's concrete evidence. However, you also need to keep in mind that in ghost hunting, it's quite

Chapter Four: How to Use the Scientific Method in Ghost Hunting

unpredictable but a lot of paranormal investigators know that there are certain places in the U.S. or even in the world that are consistent haunts or paranormal activity.

The further steps after proving your hypothesis is to turn it into a theory, and if you're lucky enough you can make it into a law or turn it into a fact. People won't be wondering anymore if it's a possibility because they will now conclude that it is reality, that it is concrete.

You can use the scientific method to become a better and more reliable paranormal investigator or ghost hunter. Make sure to enhance your observational skills, develop your hypothesis, pay attention to details, document everything, keep testing it to the point that you will see the exact same results over and over again, and you're on your way to turning it into a theory and perhaps a law of nature.

Chapter Five: Ethics of Paranormal Investigation

Paranormal investigation is a field that draws on different kinds of field such as psychology, religion, medicine, history, journalism and other related fields. However, unlike other fields, the paranormal field doesn't have a set of formal ethical guidelines or standards of ethical conduct the way other fields do. And this is because it is still not yet established as an official field in the United States and in other parts of the world. The paranormal field is still labeled as pseudoscience, it still doesn't have institutions or

Chapter Five: Ethics of Paranormal Investigation

some form of oversight committee that will create the official guidelines, and it doesn't have a tradition like the oath – taking or board exams to qualify someone as a paranormal investigator.

Unfortunately, there are also no forms of venues to talk about the ethical issues of paranormal investigations either, and it's probably because it's quite easy to assume that if you are a skeptic paranormal investigator, then you are the one who reveals the truth and defends clients or people from getting scammed and fooled by con artists pretending they can talk to ghosts or carry out paranormal investigations. So it's quite easy to assume that since a skeptic is on the right side, then there's no need for ethical guidelines because you are all about helping people but there's also the fact that even if your intention is good, it doesn't mean that all the different means of your investigation is proper.

It's like if you're a surgeon, and your intention is to do everything to save your patient's life, but you should still abide a certain code of conduct when you're doing the

Chapter Five: Ethics of Paranormal Investigation

surgery, or provide the patient with the right opportunities for treatment and perhaps not withheld any information.

Deception

Deception is one of the most common methods used by paranormal investigators, and it's very unavoidable and understandable why it is the go – to premise of most ghost hunters. Many investigators have to go undercover (just like how FBI folks do) or needless to say, lied about who they are and why they're there and why they need to talk to eye witnesses etc. Most ghost hunters agree that while it is unavoidable to lie when it comes to their identity or true intention, they are also aware that there could be a potential of misuse, or how far one can go when it comes to deceiving people just so they can get access and information from their target.

There are paranormal investigators who have developed their own code of conduct when it comes to setting the boundaries of deception which is good because you or your team have to figure out before you go out in the field and do anything what you are willing and not willing

Chapter Five: Ethics of Paranormal Investigation

to do otherwise it's very easy to just tolerate unethical behavior which can affect your crew's reputation and perhaps safety.

What other paranormal investigators do to somehow mitigate deception to some degree is to debrief their targets after the fact. You may want to tell them that you lied about something, how and why. This is also aligned with the code of conduct being used by certain fields in psychology, or certain psychological researchers (or any other researchers for this matter) also use whenever they're conducting an experiment or trying to acquire information from different subjects. You can deceive your subjects or eye witnesses to some extent but you may need to tell them the truth after doing it.

Chapter Six: Paranormal Investigation Proper

A haunting is a recurring presence of a ghost, demon, or any supernatural element or being at a specific location. A haunting can happen anywhere. People all over the world believe in ghosts and haunting and recorded throughout history. There have been anthropological evidences that indicates it was common even in pre – historic times. Typical ghost researchers usually consist of paranormal investigators, anthropologists, folklorists, parapsychologists, historian, and of course, skeptics. In this chapter, you'll learn

Chapter Six: Paranormal Investigation Proper

the different types of haunting or perhaps you can also call it as types of conscious energy that you will most likely encounter in the paranormal field.

Intelligent

This kind of entity is aware of its environment including the living human beings who are present within the location or area. The entity can be classified as benevolent, benign or malevolent which is something we're going to discuss a little later.

Residual

It is believed that a residual haunting happens when a ghost visits the same location and performs a repetitive act. The ghost is not cognizant of any living humans who are present within the area, and often times is not totally aware of its environment as we see it today. Residual haunting usually happens after a tragic event, say an accident or a fire, and the repetitive acts displays a portion of the event that happened. Sometimes the residual effect is of a mundane act the individual repeated often in life like a really rigid

Chapter Six: Paranormal Investigation Proper

routine. Generally these kinds of entities aren't considered as ghosts but instead a spiritual imprint or residual energy left at the location just like what we've discussed in the first few chapters of the book.

Classification of Ghosts

Ghosts and other form of spiritual entities can be classified under three categories: Benevolent, Benign, and Malevolent.

Benevolent

This type of haunting is of a protective nature. It is usually felt that the ghost or conscious energy is a loved one looking to protect the living people within an area in which a demon or other possibly malevolent entity exists. These types of ghosts are often found to be related to the living people within the area but have also been found to be closely connected to those being attacked.

Benign

Chapter Six: Paranormal Investigation Proper

This type of haunting usually happens when the ghost is unconcerned with the living or perhaps unaware of their presence in the location. This type of ghost can also be connected to an intelligent conscious energy or residual energy.

<u>Malevolent</u>

This type of ghost usually happens when a powerful conscious energy or perhaps a malevolent spiritual entity like a demon seeks to inflict harm on the living within an area. It is believed that this happens because the ghost is angry about the events that may have occurred in its life. It may also have a malicious personality, is jealous of the living, or an entity who is seeking attention or being defensive of its home and wishes for the current people living there to leave, or it is sad and want others to acknowledge its misery and sadness.

Poltergeist activities is usually confused with a malevolent haunting but often times it's a spirit seeking attention or asking for help. A demon can be present if a murder occurred in the area. These types of haunting exist but they are very rare. You can study demonology so that you'll have a basic understanding as to how it can be related to paranormal phenomena.

Tips Before Leaving the House

A lot of the information you'll read in this chapter is mainly just plain common sense but you would be surprised at how many paranormal investigators forget the basic things before they go out in the field. Y

Tip #1: Make sure to list all the equipment you plan on using with you for your paranormal investigation.

You might even plan the items you will bring based on the location you're going to investigate – if it is either indoor or outdoor. Make sure that all your equipment is in good shape, fully charged, or you that you have extra batteries, power cords, backup memory card etc. Battery draining is usually common when investigating since ghosts are usually conscious energy that can harness the power in your batteries. You also want to make sure that you have

Chapter Six: Paranormal Investigation Proper

lens cleaning cloth for your camera / camcorder lenses this is because there are some locations that are dusty, or especially if you are outdoors, you can be facing some dirt – filled areas. You don't want to cause some confusion when you're reviewing your documentation later. It's a good idea to also label your equipment with a label marker so that in the instance that you accidentally left it somewhere it can be returned to you.

Tip #2: Make sure your cell phone is fully charged

While it's not ideal to carry your phone while you're doing an investigation as it can disrupt the frequency of the other pieces of equipment and also cause false positives. However, it's of course ideal to have just in case of an emergency. Just make sure that it's turned off during your sessions.

Chapter Six: Paranormal Investigation Proper

Tip #3: Consider your clothing for paranormal investigation

You need to wear appropriate clothing depending on where you're going to conduct the investigation. You need to also consider if it's indoors or outdoors. Is it cold or warm? Is it rainy? Make sure to check the weather in the location you're going to and plan accordingly. If it's cold outside then consider dressing in layers to stay warm but make sure to avoid wearing any clothing that might rub and cause noise. You may also consider wearing a windbreaker clothing so that it wouldn't interfere with your EVP sessions if you are outside walking and recording. You might also consider packing foot warmers, hand warmers or a bonnet. You may also want to consider bringing insect repellant, bug spray or boots. You may want to consider wearing clothing with lots of pockets to help you hold items or you can also wear a hunter's vest. Rubber shoes are ideal for any location since it will help you get a decent grip on the surfaces and at the same time your feet will be protected.

If you're conducting an investigation in an abandoned building, you need to make sure that your feet are protected since there could be a lot of debris in the building. You shouldn't also wear jewelries, or have keys that will dangle and make noise that can potentially contaminate your EVP session. You shouldn't also use any kind of cologne or perfume because there are some spirits that like to emit odors and fragrances to make their presence known. You don't want to ruin the experience by wearing a scent that can be confused with the paranormal. Bottom line is to dress for your location.

Tip #4: Bring medication and first – aid kit

Make sure that the first aid kit has additional medications that you or your crew may need during an emergency. You need to also consider if you need to bring a chair or perhaps a cooler full of water as well as some food especially if you're going to stay in the location for a long period of time. Some of the paranormal investigators prefer drinking an energy drink and eat something before going in or while you/ your crew is setting up the base. Make sure that your first aid kit has hand sanitizer including dust masks, bandages, pain reliever, antibiotic ointment, gauze

Chapter Six: Paranormal Investigation Proper

and the likes. You might also consider bringing in tissues, paper towels and other appropriate items you need for any investigation location.

Tip #5: Bring a notebook and a pen!

You don't want to just rely on your equipment because it may fail to record everything. You want to have your own notebook and pen (lots of them!) so that you can take notes on your location and you'll also have reference once you get on the site. Note everything you see, hear or feel within the specific location but also be open minded to encountering other spirits or ghosts as they may show up everywhere or get around the location.

Tip #6: Be prepared!

You want to always have a contingency plan, and consider every worst case scenario that can happen on your way to the site, during and after the investigation. Check your vehicle if it has a good spare of tire and jack in the event that a flat tire happens. Have a jumper cable in case your car battery goes out. Check the gas, the car's condition, insurance for you and your team, GPS system, and other logistics. Say for example, it's going to be a long trip to the location; you also want to consider checking a reasonable hotel so you can get some rest on the road. Have everything you need such as clothing, toiletries, food and water, credit cards etc. Additionally, if you become sick, you should know where the nearest hospital is or have an emergency contact. Make sure you have a list of phone numbers with names to call just in case an emergency happens. If you took medications, you should note it in a paper and keep it somewhere where your team can find it like a wallet along with other identification.

Ghost Haunting Basics

Step #1: Get permission.

Before you step foot on any property, you have to make sure that you have the written permission or perhaps explicit permission from the owner or caretaker of the property to conduct your investigation. It's better if you also have the owner/ caretaker sign a waiver form.

Chapter Six: Paranormal Investigation Proper

Step #2: Always investigate with your team

You should never go on a paranormal investigation alone. This is because things could get out of hand not just on a physical but also on a spiritual level. Make sure that you have at least a partner or preferably a group at all times. Carry a cell phone at all times but be sure to turn it off or put it in silent mode during your sessions.

Step #3: Do your homework

As elaborately mentioned in previous chapters, you need to do your research first before you go to your target location. You need to know the history of the place (both current and its past if any) and also do background checks on the people who currently own the property as well as the previous owner. You need to also do prior interview with the people around the area who may have had paranormal experiences at the location. Be prepared to do some debunking.

Chapter Six: Paranormal Investigation Proper

Step #4: Make sure that all your equipment is ready to go

Make sure that the equipment is fully charged, have cleaned lenses, working audio or metric, and that you have extra batteries and/ or memory storage. You need to also pack it in your bag properly to prevent damage and for it to be free of debris etc. Ensure that you have fresh recording supplies for both your video and audio equipment. You don't want to run out of storage space when the paranormal activity is taking place. As mentioned in previous chapters, it is not necessary to have very expensive equipment to start your investigation. You just need to have the basics including a flashlight, digital voice recorder, digital camera, video recorder, extra microphone and other basic sound enhancement computer program for reviewing EVPs.

Step #5: Be positive

As you now know, the conscious energy or the ghost you may encounter may either be benign or malevolent. You want to promote a positive energy and be respectful of the deceased as well. If you respect the ghost, you will have

Chapter Six: Paranormal Investigation Proper

better chances of getting a response from the ghost since they are not threatened or something.

Step #6: Do a preliminary investigation

You might want to do a quick sweep of the location before you begin the investigation proper. You can also take photos for comparison purposes later on when you are already reviewing your findings. Keep in mind that you should focus more on the specific area where haunting have been reported. You don't need to investigate to all the areas; you can still do so but you should start to where the action is.

Step #7: Don't smoke or get drunk prior or during your investigation

Cigarette smoke is usually the cause of a false anomaly so you should avoid smoking whenever you're conducting your investigation. Obviously, you don't want to come in drunk because it will just ruin your credibility as a paranormal investigator/ expert.

Chapter Six: Paranormal Investigation Proper

Step #8: Write it down

Make sure to take notes of what you see, feel or hear before during and even after your investigation. In addition to this, take note if you have contaminated evidence (such as if that moment, someone cough or sneeze etc.) so that you can debunk the sounds later once you review the documentation.

Step #9: Never wear cologne or a distinct scent

Generally, there are some paranormal beings that will let their presence known by simply emitting some kind of fragrance. Friendly entities usually give off a pleasant scent while malevolent spirits will emit foul odors.

Step #10: Never form a conclusion on – site.

You want to closely review and analyze your evidences first and even go back to your hypothesis before you make a conclusion. You also would most likely need to do a follow – up investigation and see if you can trigger the ghost to

Chapter Six: Paranormal Investigation Proper

appear again, and keep testing to also answer questions that may come up while reviewing your findings.

Arrival on Location

You and your team arrive on the location excited and ready to go. Now what you need to do first is to simply relax, take a deep breath and focus. You need to prepare your things, set up your base (if need be), decide what to bring inside and what you can come back for later, and do an initial sweep first.

Most locations especially if it's a private residence, you will have somebody greet you; the owner or caretaker might instruct you where to stay out of, what electrical outlets you can use, where you can set up a base or leave your stuff etc. Make sure to follow and respect them. Ask any questions beforehand if need be. You might also want to ask if you can get a quick tour of the location especially if it's a big property so that you'll have an idea of how big the place is, where to go etc. Don't forget to take photos during the tour so that you can do some comparison when you get to review your evidences later on. There are some locations

Chapter Six: Paranormal Investigation Proper

where you need to sign a liability waiver as well. Keep in mind, listen to what you're told and be polite and show respect especially if you need to interview them.

If you're working with a team on – site you may have already decided how the crew will be split up for the investigation. If not, you can do so after the site tour or during the walk – through would be a good time to assign who will be responsible for each task and how you as a team will approach the investigation. You should preferably have a team leader/s where you can report and/ or do some decision – making especially in the event of an emergency.

This is also the time to pull out your recorders and go around having each member of the crew say their name in a regular tone of voice followed by a whisper so that later on you are ready with the tagging of audio files when your review your findings.

Before you can conduct your paranormal investigation, I highly recommend that you say your prayers of protection. No one of course should be forced to join in but everyone should be respectful of those participating in the team prayer regardless of religion or belief.

Chapter Seven: Paranormal Investigation Techniques

Paranormal investigations like any other fields take time, patience and a lot of work. Don't expect to see or hear anything at first when you start your investigation but make sure to have your equipment turned on because it doesn't mean that if you go back to see the photos and listen to your audio recordings that you won't find anything. Hunting ghosts is not like what you see on movies or TV wherein you get a continuous paranormal activity this is why you and

Chapter Seven: Destiny Expression Numbers 5, 6, 7, 8 and 9

your team have to be very patient because paranormal activity is very rare, so if you experience one, double down on it.

If your intent in participating in a paranormal investigation is to have a ghost scare you or even chase you, then you should just stay home and rent a horror movie. True paranormal investigators are people that are dedicated to the craft and the research that goes with it. If you're the type of person who easily gets startled, screams or freaks out then you shouldn't be in this field because it can be a major distraction and it can also contaminate the evidence that the team will gather. Save your teammates the headache and leave it for those who are serious in researching for paranormal activity.

Be a Skeptic and Do Some Debunking First

Make sure to focus on the investigation and always do some debunking first before you jump to false conclusions. If something happens during the investigation (physical or paranormal), keep your cool and have a peace of

Chapter Seven: Destiny Expression Numbers 5, 6, 7, 8 and 9

mind so that you will know what to do. Debunk the activity first and consider environmental factors. For instance, if there's a sound, you might want to check where it is coming from, and if there's other factors like the weather, a loose screw etc. If you felt something, could it have been your clothing getting caught on something or a perhaps a crew member brushing by you? This is how you debunk any unusual activity or possible anomaly.

Once you have ruled out all outside factors, you can then start asking the ghost or conscious energy random questions. Communicate to the ghost and see if you get a response. Keep in mind that once you start communicating, you need to keep taking photos and the camcorders should already be rolling. Make sure that you have turned on the digital voice recorder and other equipment like EMF readers, thermo readers or thermo – imaging if you have one. Start asking questions in line with the recent paranormal activity done. For instance, "did you throw that object?" "could you knock like me?" (Knock on something so that the ghost can imitate you). Make sure to speak in a

Chapter Seven: Destiny Expression Numbers 5, 6, 7, 8 and 9

normal voice, if somewhat quiet tone when doing your EVP session.

Be aware of your surroundings. What floor of the house or the building are you on? Do you feel any drafts from hallways, doors or windows? Where is the nearest exit? Where are your team members? What normal activities are taking place at the moment? Keep in mind, never go off alone.

Make sure to never provoke the ghost or spirits that is present. Try to say something or try to do something normal that might trigger a reaction. For instance, if you're in a church, you can stand at the lectern and maybe read a verse from the Bible and see if you get a reaction. If you're in a hospital, you might want to do some reenactment or pretend to be a patient needing help, or do anything that could recreate the scenario that happened on that particular area based on your eye witnesses or your research. If you hear music playing and you recognize the tune, you can perhaps sing a little bit of the song and see if you can get the ghost to interact with you.

Chapter Seven: Destiny Expression Numbers 5, 6, 7, 8 and 9

If you have a reader with you, don't depend on them to lead you straight to the where the ghost is.

Different equipment usually works on different frequencies, and while it may pick up something in one area, it may not necessarily pick up everything on the location. If you are using more than one medium, they may pick up on different things on the area where they may not necessarily match up. This is because each of them has different function and picks up on different frequencies, which is why it's very important that you know what they are and why you need to use them at that particular moment or location. This goes back to what we've discussed earlier in using the scientific method. You need to create a hypothesis and match the equipment you need to test out your idea.

Chapter Seven: Destiny Expression Numbers 5, 6, 7, 8 and 9

Chapter Eight: EVP Sessions

EVP or Electronic Voice Phenomenon is recordings of voice or voice – like sounds that aren't usually audible to the human ear. The frequencies of the sounds that are usually produced is well below the range of decibels that can be perceived by the human ear. EVPs typically (though not always) are short and it has a length of a short phrase or just one word. Paranormal investigators on the field uses a digital voice recorder during the EVP sessions, and it's highly recommended that investigators bring at least two to

Chapter Eight: EVP Sessions

three recorders; one that you can keep on you and begin recording on from the time you arrive at the location until you leave, while the other one or two is used for EVP burst sessions, and also sessions as a stationery recording in a particular area.

The additional digital recorders will allow you to see if you have capture anything different that the other one or two didn't. It's also a great idea for review or backup especially when you hear something on one equipment so that you and your team can check or cross – reference it on the other digital recording. Below are ways on how to capture EVPs and how they can be classified:

Capturing EVPs

Tip #1: Make sure to have extra batteries on hand for your digital voice recorder/s

Tip #2: If you're going to say something, make sure to never whisper and speak clearly. If for instance, your eye witness is saying something on a low tone, make sure to audibly

Chapter Eight: EVP Sessions

notate it on your recording to avoid confusion later on when you're reviewing the EVPs.

Tip #3: Ensure that your recorder is away from your mouth. Again, this is to avoid confusion, you don't want to breathe in to the recorder and mistake that as a sound produced by a ghost.

Tip #4: Turn off your phone or at least put it into silent mode during your EVP session.

Tip #5: Keep your phone away from the equipment as it could throw frequency distortions on tape recorders, video cameras and also EMF meters.

Tip #6: When you start your EVP session, you need to catalog as much information as possible on your recording:

- Make sure to state the time
- Make sure to state the location (for instance what room or floor number you are in etc.)
- Make sure to note how many people are in the room during the time that you and your team are conducting a session

Chapter Eight: EVP Sessions

- Make sure that you and all your team members as well as all the people present state their name so that you can have a reference later to their voices.

Tip #7: When it comes to providing information, be as specific as possible and pay attention to the details of what you're describing.

Tip #8: Don't let anything hit the recorder such as other piece of equipment, your clothing, the lens cap or anything else.

Tip #9: You can talk during the EVP session is okay as long as you don't talk over other people whenever they're speaking so that later on you can distinguish clearly the voices on the EVP recordings.

Tip #10: You need to also audibly note any sound heard including notating sneezes, sniffles, cough, shuffling of feet, scratches etc.

Tip #11: Don't wear or carry noisy items that can do clinking sounds such as loose jewelries, keys, pocket coins etc.

Tip #12: You also want to record in short session to make reviewing sound bites easier.

Chapter Eight: EVP Sessions

Tip #13: Ask the ghost a simple question and allow at least twenty seconds for an answer. This is because since ghosts are conscious energy, they will most likely draw energy from other sources in order to communicate to you which is why it may take a while for them to respond.

Tip #14: Keep in mind, there may be other ghosts that are all around within an area so don't get too attached to just one that you forget to communicate to the others.

Sample Questions to Ask

Below are some ideas of questions you would want to ask during your EVP session. You can be creative and focus your questions around topics that you've learned when you did your research for that particular investigation.

- Are you a male or female?
- What is your name?
- Are you married?
- Can you make a noise like this (do something that the ghost may imitate like knocking on an object etc.)
- Can we take a photo of you?

Chapter Eight: EVP Sessions

- What year is it?
- Do you know you're dead?
- Do you want to leave this place?
- Why do you like it here?
- Do you want me/ us to pray for you?
- Do you have any message that you like us to pass along to someone?

Keep in mind that friendly ghosts are more willing to talk to you when you are giving off a positive energy. You can experiment and also take turns when asking questions especially if there are members of the opposite sex on your team. Sometimes ghosts respond to one gender over another. You don't want to threaten or yell on the ghost because even if they are friendly, they could get angry and do you harm. Make sure to ask simple and short question – less is more. You can ask around 3 to 4 questions then leave, if the ghost has more to say, they will let you know.

A few more tips, if for instance, there's an occurrence such as someone bumps a furniture or the sound of a car

Chapter Eight: EVP Sessions

pulling up outside, make to vocally mark it in the recorder by saying something like: "Note, we heard a loud thump in the third floor above us after asking this question." You might think that the simple things aforementioned can be easily remembered but you'll be surprised later on what you might forget, so keep a checklist and tick the boxes each time so that you don't overlook anything.

Classification of EVPs

There are several different classifications of EVPs and it can fall into any of the four categories: Class A, B, C and Class R.

Class A

For an EVP to be classified under Class A, the audio must have a very clear voice and everyone who will listen to the playback will agree on what is being said without being told by someone else. It should be pretty clear for everyone. Class A EVPs don't need to be cleared up or amplified using a computer sound editing program anymore because it be clearly heard through the raw output. It doesn't have to be loud, but the words should be clear. The EVPs under Class A category are the best voices of the ghosts captured but unfortunately it's also the rarest to record.

Class B

A Class B EVP is somewhat similar to Class A with just a slight difference. It can be understood and most people will agree on what is being said but it may not be understood by everyone who listens to it and it might even sound like it's saying something completely different from some other people. Class B EVPs usually need the aid of an amplifier or a computer sound enhancement program before it can be clearly understood by everyone. For this classification, the voice can just be fairly clear and most words are easy to determine especially once it's already analyzed by the computer. This is the most common class of EVP to be captured.

Chapter Eight: EVP Sessions

Class C

Class C EVPs are the worst type of quality voice recording that a paranormal investigator can capture. This is because it's nearly impossible to understand what is being said even when aided with a computer sound enhancement program. These types are often whispers or just mumbled words that can even sound robotic at time. The voice can't be understood but you will still know that it's an EVP because of the fact that it is the only one talking during the recording session, and perhaps human sounding voices can only be clearly heard in the background.

Class R

A Class R rating means that the recording can have a meaning when it's played on reverse. Some audios have a meaning when it's played normally, but a different meaning in reverse. When this happens, the EVP can be classified under two categories. For instance, a Class A EVP with excellent and clear meaning in reverse as well will receive a Class A – RA rating. This means that it was very clear to

Chapter Eight: EVP Sessions

understand both forward and in reverse. It can also have a Class A – RC rating which can mean that it couldn't be understood in reverse causing it to not be a Class R EVP. You may have a Class A – RB or a Class B – RB.

Chapter Nine: Additional Ghost Hunting Tips

When it comes to taking photos, more experienced photographers can most probably give you a better idea of the technicalities of cameras, flashes, angles and the likes but we will not go over those topics in this book. However, if you want to learn more about these types of topics, I highly suggest that you contact a local photographer near you who

Chapter Nine: Additional Ghost Hunting Tips

is not linked with paranormal investigations to give you a wholesome tips and tricks.

You can also watch a couple of tutorials on YouTube especially on learning about avoiding false positives or false anomalies which usually happens with the photographic evidences.

As previously mentioned, when you initially arrive on the site, make sure to take lots of photos of the location or the area before you start conducting your paranormal investigation. These photos will be essential to your review process once you get home so that you can compare it back to them especially when you think you have caught something during the sessions. This is a very important step in debunking.

When you or one of your team members is taking photos, always keep in mind the 1, 2, 3 Rule – take 3 photos in a row when you're taking pictures of the location. The importance of this is that it will give you a chance to see if there would be any movement as well as sudden appearance or disappearance. Make sure to watch where your fingers

Chapter Nine: Additional Ghost Hunting Tips

are on the camera because sometimes we don't notice that our fingers are blocking the shot or the flash. You'd be surprised how many investigators think they have caught a shadow figure in a photo only to realize it was just the tip of their finger blocking the flash. You need to also be aware of wearing caps or bulky form of clothing as it can sometimes create a shadow. Make sure to tuck away any neck straps, camera cords or anything else that can sway or swing into the photo. Don't worry about reviewing photos as you go unless of course you saw something with your own eyes; otherwise you might lose the opportunity to take a snap at the paranormal activity around you. You can maybe review them after a couple of shots just to quickly see if you got that photo.

Photo and Video Tips

Below are some tips to keep in mind whenever you are taking photos or even shooting a video:

Chapter Nine: Additional Ghost Hunting Tips

Tip #1: Avoid taking photos or videos during any kind of weather conditions especially if smoke is visible, or there's a heavy fog as it can definitely contaminate your findings.

Tip #2: Make sure to hold your breath when taking photos on a cold night to avoid mistaking your breath as a ghostly figure.

Tip #3: Make sure to hold the camera still as movement will surely distort the photo and can contaminate your evidences.

Tip #4: Never take photos of reflective or shiny items because it can easily be mistaken as something "ghostly" unless of course the ghost actually chooses to appear there like in a mirror.

Tip #5: Make sure that you know what your camera or video recorder can and can't capture. You should test it out before you do any investigation.

Tip #6: Don't take video or photos that are against the light as it can create a glare and definitely destroy any possible evidence you may have. Always try to find the best angle or

Chapter Nine: Additional Ghost Hunting Tips

see if you can position yourself in places where the shot will be clear without a shooting barrier of some sort.

Tricks of the Trade

In addition to the typical equipment and techniques aforementioned, there are some tricks to keep in mind that can be handy during your investigation:

- A tape measure or a dollar bill can be handy as it can be a reference to the size of something or for movement. You can easily place something like a ball at the end of the tape measure and ask the ghost if he/she can move the ball. Leave to conduct your research in another area and then come back a little later to see if there is any movement.

- You can use flour or baby powder if you want to catch footsteps. Make sure to bring a black plastic table cloth or a tarp to use for this so that you won't mess up the location of the client. You can sprinkle the powder down on the table cloth or tarp

Chapter Nine: Additional Ghost Hunting Tips

throughout the night, then come back to see if there's any footprints or if has been disturbed. If you capture something, use the dollar bill beside it then take a photo so that you and your team will have an idea of the size.

- Flashlights are handy tricks of the trade that lots of professional paranormal investigators used. Flashlights aren't only used for safety or finding your way in the dark but it can also function as communication devices by simply turning it off and on, and ask the ghost to contact you through turning the flashlight off and on. Make sure that the flashlight you use doesn't turn on easily through vibrations of thing like an aircon. Sometimes, you would want to use a couple of flashlights so always have more than one on hand that's all fully charged and bring extra batteries with you just in case you will need it.

- Trigger objects are also one of the most common tricks that paranormal experts use to make the ghost

Chapter Nine: Additional Ghost Hunting Tips

communicate. You can bring items like balloons, toys, tools, balls or something that the ghost may resonate with according to your research. It will also work for children ghosts since they can be drawn to such items, and they may even interact with you through these trigger objects.

Dowsing rods can be quite tricky but some still use them. You first have to establish what positions will be used for a yes, neutral and no responses which is why it's much harder to do. What happens is that the crew uses the rods pointing straight forward as neutral, pointing away as no, and crossing as a yes response. However, you need to make sure that you asked a controlled question in order to determine whether you're dealing with an intelligent conscious energy or not; something like asking if the ghost's middle name is Walker or something similar to ensure that the ghost answers correctly. Make sure to keep your hands steady when conducting a dowsing rod session. There could be instances where ghosts will be quite playful and you would

Chapter Nine: Additional Ghost Hunting Tips

see how they will twirl the rods round and round just make sure you capture all of it on video.

Chapter Ten: Prayers of Protection

If you and your team choose to say prayers before and after conducting paranormal investigation, below you can find prayers that you can do before and after you investigate. We suggest that all prayers be said in a circle with all team members while all of you are holding hands. Concentration on the words of the prayers plus positive energy is essential so that the prayer will maintain its power. You don't have to include everyone on your team especially if they are of other religious practices but please respect the

Chapter Ten: Prayers of Protection

ones who will do. The prayers mentioned here are taken from National Paranormal Society's Guide to Paranormal Investigating. You can create your own set of prayers depending on your religion or what you think can help you so that you and your team members can have a spiritual protection.

Prayers Before the Investigation

St. Michael's Prayer

Saint Michael the archangel, defend us in battle. Be our protection against the wickedness and snares of the devil. May God rebuke him, we humbly pray. And do thou, O prince of the heavenly host, by the power of God, thrust into hell Satan and all evil spirits who wander through the world for the ruin of souls. Amen.

Calm Protection Prayer Prior

Heavenly Father, we gather here tonight as investigators to better understand the universe you have given us. We ask you to watch over us, to guide us and keep our minds focused and free from fear. We ask for your protection from any that would do us harm and hope you will give understanding to those we seek, assuring them of our intent and that they have nothing to fear from us as investigators. Again we ask you to see us safely through this night. Amen

Strong Protection Prayer Prior

Our Heavenly Father, we come to this location tonight to better understand the unknown. We do, as investigators, know that there are dangers in searching for these truths. We come to you and ask you to protect our hearts, minds, bodies, and souls from any and all inhuman, malevolent, foul, or evil spirits. We call on your Arch Angel Michael to stand by our sides. We ask your guidance, so we may get through this night safely without harm to your children on either side. We once again ask that you protect us from all harm and danger. Amen.

Chapter Ten: Prayers of Protection

Prayer Before the Hunt

May we be strong in the Lord and in the strength of his Might! St. Michael, the archangel, shall defund us and be our protection against all evil and negativity on all levels. May the Divine light of the Archangels and all the Ascended masters surround us with their love. We call on Metatron and ask that all negative thought forms, lost souls, negative residues, negative elementals, and fragments be permanently healed and taken into the light, that all may be freed according to the highest will of God. May we be purified and blessed upon every level of our being, in the work we do, and be given more Divine power and protection. Thy will be done! Thank you and Amen.

Prayers After the Investigation

Closing Prayer

In the name of Jesus Christ, I command all human spirits to be bound to the confines of the cemetery. I command all inhuman spirits to go where Jesus Christ tells you to go, for it is he who commands you. Amen.

Chapter Ten: Prayers of Protection

Calm Protection Prayer After

Lord, thank you for seeing us safely through this investigation. We brought no spirits with us and ask you let none follow us from this location, other than the loved ones we carry with us always. Finally, we ask for your continued protection to see us safely home. Amen.

Strong Protection Prayer After

We are speaking to any and all entities who have chosen to follow us out of this location. We command all human and inhuman spirits whom want to follow us home to stay at this location. You are not allowed to attach to us or our equipment. We bind you to this location and command you to return to where you came from. We do this with the authority Christ gave us. Heavenly Father, we ask you see us safely from this location and protect us on our journey. Amen.

Chapter Ten: Prayers of Protection

Simple Closing Prayer

In the name of Jesus Christ, I command all human spirits to be bound to the confines of the cemetery. I command all inhuman spirits to go where Jesus Christ tells you to go, for it is he who commands you. Amen.

Closing Prayer

God bless every corner of this house, may peace dwell within. Protect all that come and go, whether friend or kin. Bless every door and window pane, and every ceiling and wall. Bless every closet, nook and cranny, crawl space or basement, bless it all! Bless the roof and ground surrounding with your protective love and light. Hold us in your love care every second of every day, in every way from early morning into sheltered night. Let all be in your complete perfection as you intended. Release all negativity into your confirmed light that is extended. We thank you and expect your miraculous intervention. Clearing all with purification, love, peach and joy as divinely intended. Amen

Chapter Ten: Prayers of Protection

Protection Prayers

This should be said after an opening prayer.

Pre - Investigation Prayer of Protection

Heavenly Father, God of the Universe, we all come to you in prayer tonight for our protection. Please protect our bodies, souls, equipment, and all personal possessions from any harm. We ask that you send your angels to guard us against all evil and malevolent spirits and protect us with your white light. We give permission to your angels to intervene for us on our behalf. We pray that you allow the spirits to show themselves to us and allow us to obtain evidence of their existence. Lord, let our endeavors tonight not be in vain. Please allow us to have a safe an eventful investigation tonight. We pray that no spirit or ghost, of evil will or intention, be allowed to attach themselves to any of us or our belongings and that they not be allowed to follow us to our homes or enter therein. We pray Lord that you also protect all of our fellow paranormal investigators from any

Chapter Ten: Prayers of Protection

harm tonight and allow us all a safe journey to our homes. We pray these things in the name of the Father, the Son (Jesus Christ) and the Holy Spirit. Amen.

Simple Protection Prayer

Visit Lord we pray this place, and drive from it all the snares of the enemy, let your holy angels dwell here to keep us in peace, and may your blessing be upon it evermore through Jesus hrist our Lord. Amen.

The Hedge Prayer

Trusting in the promise that whatever we ask the Father in Jesus' name he will do, we now approach you, Father, with the confidence in our Lord's words and in your infinite power and love for us. With the intercession of the blessed Virgin Mary, mother of God, the blessed apostles Peter and Paul, the blessed Archangel Michael, our guardian angels, all the Saints and Angels in Heaven, and holy in the power of his blessed name, we ask you Father to protect us and keep us from the harassment of the devil and his minions. Father, we ask that you build a Hedge of Protection

Chapter Ten: Prayers of Protection

around us and to help keep the hedge repaired and the gates locked so that the devil and his minions have no access or means to breach the hedge except by your expressed will. Father we know that we are powerless against the spiritual forces of evil and recognize our utter dependence on you and your power. Look with mercy upon us. Do not look upon our sins, O Lord; rather look at the sufferings of your beloved Son and see the victim whose bitter passion and death has reconciled us to you. By the victory of the cross, protect us from all evil and rebuke any evil spirits who wish to attack, influence, or breach your Hedge of Protection in any way. Send them back to Hell and fortify your hedge for our protection by the blood of your Son, Jesus. Send your Holy Angels to watch over us and protect us. Father, all of these things we ask in the most holy name of Jesus Christ, your Son. Thank you Father for hearing our prayer. Amen.

Ring of Protection Prayer

In the name of all that is goodness and light, surround our circle in the white light of holy protection. We ask that no harm befalls or follows the protected circle and that our

quest benefit all who are among us. In the name of all that is goodness and light, we thank thee for your protection of holy white light.
Amen.

Ground Blessing

Our help is in the name of the Lord who has made heaven and earth. The Lord be will you and with your spirit. Let us pray. Lord God almighty, bless this land. May health, chastity, conquest of sin, virtue, humility, goodness, and meekness flourish here. May the law be observed in its fullness, and thanks be given to God the Father, and the Son, and the Holy Spirit. And may this blessing always remain on this land and on those who live in it, now and forever and ever. Amen.

St. Christopher Prayer for Travelers/Prayer for a Safe Journey

Lord, we humbly ask you to give your Almighty protection to all travelers. Accept our fervent and sincere prayers that through your great power and unfaltering

Chapter Ten: Prayers of Protection

spirit, those who travel may reach their destination safe and sound. Grant your divine guidance and infinite wisdom to all who operate automobiles, trains, planes and boats. Inspire them with due sense of duty and knowledge and help them guide those entrusted in their care to complete their travel safely. We thank you, oh Lord, for your great mercy and unending love to all mankind and for extending your arm of protection to all travelers. Amen.

Chapter Ten: Prayers of Protection

Glossary of Paranormal Terms

Anomaly – an unusual or irregular event that doesn't fit the standard law or rule; it is something that can't be explained by existing accepted scientific theories. Anything abnormal, odd, weird, difficult to classify or strange can be considered as an anomaly.

Anthropomorphic – ascribing human form or characteristics of a being or thing that's not human like a deity that's resembling or made to resemble a human form.

Apophenia – it is the spontaneous perception of meaning and connections of unrelated occurrence.

Apparition – it is the appearance of a spirit or an unknown being.

Aura – this is invisible to the naked eye. It can be described as a certain glow that surrounds a person and changes form or color depending on the physical and mental well – being of the individual.

Automatic Writing – this is when a person can write something that's not coming from them or not their own writing style. This usually happens when a deceased or a ghost use the person to convey messages.

Channeling – the method in which equipment allow itself to be used in order to manifest something which comes from outside or from a particular entity.

Clairvoyance – supernatural power of seeing places, things, events or people outside the time and space of natural viewing.

Cryptozoology – the branch of paranormal research that studies the exploration of legendary creatures such as ghosts, mysterious creatures such as Big Foot and the likes.

Déjà Vu – seeing or doing something that's completely new but having the feeling that the experienced had been done before.

Demon/Demonic – a supernatural malevolent entity that causes harm to the living and/ or extreme emotional distress.

Demonology – the study of demons

Disembodied Voice – a voice that's heard in real time but is not coming from an corporeal form.

EMF (Electro – Magnet – Field) – the electromagnetic field is a physical influence that permeates through all of space. It also arises from objects that are electrically charged, and describes one of the four fundamental forces of nature which is electromagnetism. Ghost activities can oftentimes cause changes in the EMF and it is measured by using an EMF meter. There's a theory that a high amount of electromagnetic energy can cause a paranormal activity but also a theory that these same high energy levels attract ghosts and other entities.

Empath – an individual who is sensitive to the psychic emanation of his/her environment, even to a degree of telepathically getting and experiencing the emotions of other people in proximity. A psychic empathy can be regarded as a blessing and a curse but one should learn how to have control over this psychic powers.

Entity – an entity is something that has a separate or distinct existence.

Extra Sensory Perception – this is a perception that involves awareness of information about a particular event or person that is not gained through the five senses and not deducible from any previous experience.

Evil – this refers to the ethically or morally objectionable behavior or thought.

EVP (Electronic Voice Phenomena) – it is the recordings of voice or voice – like sounds that aren't usually audible to the human ear. The frequencies of the sounds that are usually produced is well below the range of decibels that can be perceived by the human ear. It can fall into any of the four categories: Class A, B, C and Class R.

> **Class A:** For an EVP to be classified under Class A, the audio must have a very clear voice and everyone who will listen to the playback will agree on what is being said without being told by someone else. It should be pretty clear for everyone. Class A EVPs don't need to be cleared up or amplified using a computer sound editing program anymore because it be clearly heard through the raw output.
>
> **Class B:** A Class B EVP is somewhat similar to Class A with just a slight difference. It can be understood and most people will agree on what is being said but

it may not be understood by everyone who listens to it and it might even sound like it's saying something completely different from some other people. Class B EVPs usually need the aid of an amplifier or a computer sound enhancement program before it can be clearly understood by everyone.

Class C: Class C EVPs are the worst type of quality voice recording that a paranormal investigator can capture. This is because it's nearly impossible to understand what is being said even when aided with a computer sound enhancement program. These types are often whispers or just mumbled words that can even sound robotic at time.

Class R: A Class R rating means that the recording can have a meaning when it's played on reverse. Some audios have a meaning when it's played normally, but a different meaning in reverse. When this happens, the EVP can be classified under two categories.

Exorcism – the practice of evicting evil spiritual entities or demons that have possessed an individual or an object. This is an ancient practice that requires mastery and shouldn't be something that is attempted by anyone except for trained clergy members.

False Positive – this is believing in something to be true when in fact is not.

Ghost – a non – corporeal manifestation or a conscious energy of an individual that has remained on Earth even after death.

Ghost Hunting – this is the act of using scientific equipment in order to detect spirits and attempt to communicate with this invisible conscious energy.

Guardian Spirit – a spirit who protects and guides a certain individual/s.

Haunting – to inhabit, appear or visit in the form of a ghost or other types of supernatural entity. There are four kinds of haunting: Intelligent, Residual, Demonic and Poltergeist.

Index

black shadows 7

Conscious Energy Theory 4

Data collecting 36

Deception 4, 50

electric 4

electromagnetic 4, 6, 7, 8, 21, 35, 36, 103

electronic voice phenomenon 6

EMF reader 21, 23, 35

energy 4, 5, 6, 7, 8, 10, 11, 12, 13, 14, 15, 16,
21, 23, 24, 29, 33, 36, 37, 39, 40, 53, 54, 55, 56, 59, 63, 70, 77, 78, 89, 90, 103, 106

equipment 1, 14, 17, 19, 22,
24, 32, 34, 38, 39, 40, 45, 56, 57, 60, 63, 68, 70, 72, 74, 75, 76, 87, 94, 96, 102, 106

ethical 48, 49

eye witness 26, 28, 30, 32, 33, 74

floating 5, 21, 36

frequency 3, 10, 11, 57, 75

ghosts 3, 1, 2, 9, 16, 17, 22, 35, 49, 52, 54, 56, 60, 68, 77, 78, 80, 89, 102, 103, 112

haunted 1, 33, 34, 35

Holographic Principle Theory 4, 15

Multiple Personality Disorder Theory 4, 8, 9

Out – of – Body Experience 4

paranormal activities 1, 16, 36

paranormal expert .... 3, 13 paranormal field 1, 2, 12, 15, 16, 42, 43, 48, 53

paranormal investigators 1, 7, 9, 12, 16, 22, 26, 47, 50, 51, 52, 56, 59, 69, 88, 96

prayers 67, 90, 99

pseudoscience 2, 42, 48

Quantum Consciousness 8, 9

questions 6, 30, 37, 39, 66, 70, 77, 78

reincarnation 9

Residual Energy 4, 11

scientific method 38, 42, 43, 47, 72

sessions 6, 21, 39, 57, 58, 62, 73, 84

skeptic 31, 49

spiritual imprinting 11, 12

theories 1, 2, 9, 16, 20, 39, 101

PHOTO REFERENCES

Page 1 Photo by user mysticartdesign via Pixabay.com

https://pixabay.com/photos/ghosts-gespenter-spooky-horror-572038/

Page 4 Photo by user AdinaVoicu via Pixabay.com

https://pixabay.com/photos/ghost-halloween-horror-bride-white-518322/

Page 18 Photo by user Lirofilmvia Pixabay.com

https://pixabay.com/photos/sony-lens-walimex-camera-1455035/

Page 26 Photo by user NeuPaddy via Pixabay.com

https://pixabay.com/photos/fog-train-lights-bill-rails-soft-1984057/

Page 43 Photo by user JordyMeow via Pixabay.com

https://pixabay.com/photos/japan-island-nagasaki-kyushu-725795/

Page 49 Photo by user JordyMeow via Pixabay.com

https://pixabay.com/photos/japan-island-nagasaki-kyushu-725796/

Page 53 Photo by user cocoparisienne via Pixabay.com

https://pixabay.com/photos/ruin-castle-ghost-weird-creepy-1837344/

Page 69 Photo by user Free – Photos via Pixabay.com

https://pixabay.com/photos/smoke-human-alone-weird-drugs-1031060/

Page 74 Photo by user stux via Pixabay.com

https://pixabay.com/photos/mixer-controller-start-226177/

Page 84 Photo by user Kellepics via Pixabay.com

https://pixabay.com/photos/fantasy-spirit-nightmare-dream-2847724/

Page 92 Photo by user Tabor via Pixabay.com

https://pixabay.com/photos/castle-mystical-mood-night-sky-1483681/

Page Photo by user Free – Photos via Pixabay.com

https://pixabay.com/photos/bible-books-god-jesus-holy-spirit-1149924/

REFERENCES

"Top 5 Ghost Hunting Mistakes" – BenjaminRadford.com

http://benjaminradford.com/wp-content/uploads/2011/11/Top-5-Ghost-Hunting-Mistakes-5.11.10.pdf

"NPS' Guide to Paranormal Investigating (aka Ghost Hunting 101)" - National-Paranormal-Society.org

http://national-paranormal-society.org/wp-content/uploads/2015/06/NPS-GH101.pdf

"How to Ghost Hunt" - GhostsandGravestones.com

https://www.ghostsandgravestones.com/how-to-ghost-hunt

"How to Actually Hunt a Ghost" – RealClearScience.com

https://www.realclearscience.com/blog/2018/01/04/how_to_actually_hunt_a_ghost.html

"The Shady Science of Ghost Hunting" – LiveScience.com

https://www.livescience.com/4261-shady-science-ghost-hunting.html

"Ghost Hunting" – CNN.com

http://edition.cnn.com/2009/TRAVEL/10/24/ghost.hunting/index.html

Ghost Hunting Gadgets – PopularMechanics.com

https://www.popularmechanics.com/technology/gadgets/a23563/ghost-hunting-gadgets/

"Chasing ghosts: the weird science of tracking the dead" – TheVerge.com

https://www.theverge.com/2012/10/31/3573206/ghost-hunters-paranormal-science-tracking-the-dead

"How to Hunt Spirits of the Dead" – HeartlandWeekend.com

http://www.heartlandweekend.com/ghost-hunting-in-asheville-2/

www.ingramcontent.com/pod-product-compliance
Lightning Source LLC
Chambersburg PA
CBHW060839050426
42453CB00008B/749